THE CHILDREN'S BOOK OF WOODWORK

THE CHILDREN'S BOOK OF WOODWORK

George Buchanan

B.T. Batsford Ltd, London

ISBN 0 7134 6122 5

Typeset by Tek-Art Ltd, Kent
and printed in Great Britain by
The Bath Press, Bath
for the publishers
B.T. Batsford Limited,
4 Fitzhardinge Street, London W1H 0AH

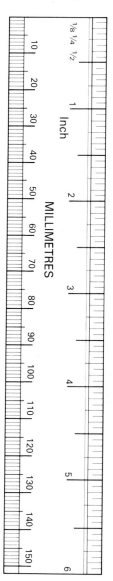

To Polly, William and James

ACKNOWLEDGMENTS

I would like to thank Polly, William and James Buchanan,
Tom Swift, Rhona and Erica MacCallum, Miles Owen and
Doug Peters for making and decorating the toys.
    I would also like to thank Peter Harding for capturing the
cover photograph, and David George for the colour
photographs. Thanks also to Ian Peters for the use of his
equipment.

This is an accurate ruler for quick
reference. If you bend the edge of the page
back, you can use it for marking out too.

CONTENTS

The Tools

Tenon Saw

This saw cuts in straight lines, and jams if you try to cut curves. It doesn't cut through metal, and its teeth will be ruined if you try.

Screwdrivers

You should have several sizes. Their blades should be ground flat and straight so they match the slots of the different screws. If the screwdriver doesn't fit, the work will be damaged.

Set Square

This is used for marking a right-angle. It has a thin metal blade. Use a knife instead of a pencil if an accurate across-the-grain sawcut is going to be made.

Fretsaw

This has a delicate blade. It can cut curves and around sharp corners. Only use a fretsaw if the wood is 6mm (¼in) thick or less. Special blades can be fitted for cutting plastic and metal.

Hammer

You will need a pin hammer to drive in the small veneer pins and gimp pins used in these projects. If massive wire nails were going to be used, then a big heavy hammer would be needed too.

Hand Drill

Turn the handcrank clockwise. Press the drill with the left hand, but don't push hard. Pull out the drill regularly to stop it jamming. Don't reverse the drill to get it out, it comes out better if the drill keeps turning in the same direction.

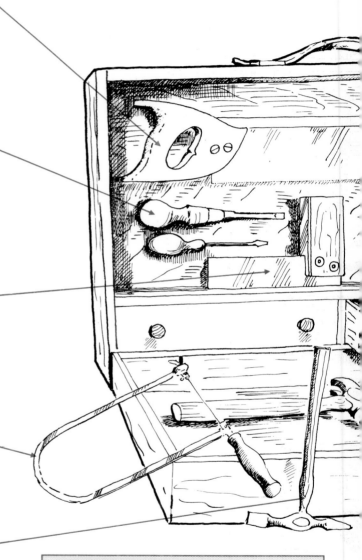

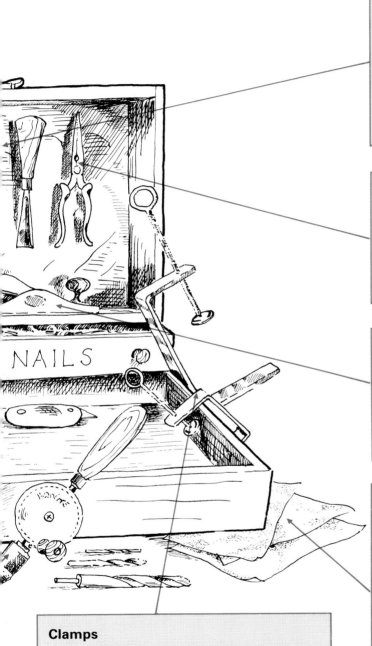

Chisel and Gouge

These have to be sharper than a razor and cut wood as though it were a lump of cheese. Protect the sharp edge with a cap, and always have both hands behind the tip of the blade. Cut away from your body, then it will be safe. The gouge must be as sharp as the chisels.

Pliers

A long-nosed pair is ideal for bending veneer pins, such as those on pulleys on the galleon. They can also be used for pulling out bent nails, and for cutting off nail heads.

Shoulder Plane

A light, small and efficient tool. It will smooth all types of wood in any direction. Try rubbing a bar of soap or a candle on to the flat sole before using the plane; it makes work much easier.

Sandpaper

You will need 90 (rough), 150 (medium) and 220 (fine) grit sandpaper. Always use a backing pad – a foam pad for smoothing curves, a felt pad with a wood backing for sanding surfaces flat. Sand diagonally across the grain. To achieve a beautiful finish, dampen the wood and leave it to dry before finally smoothing it with 220 grit paper.

Clamps

These are your extra hands, and they grip tight. With the wood clamped, sawing, planing and chiselling are easier and safer.

Chiselling

Pick up the chisel carefully.
Keep your hands behind the blade.
Keep all of your body behind tip of the chisel.
Support your work, and clamp it tightly.
Push away from you.
Leave your chisels where they can't roll off the table.

Chopping with a Chisel

Make sure there is a board underneath. Press, with the weight of your body leaning on to the right hand. Position the cutting edge with the left hand.

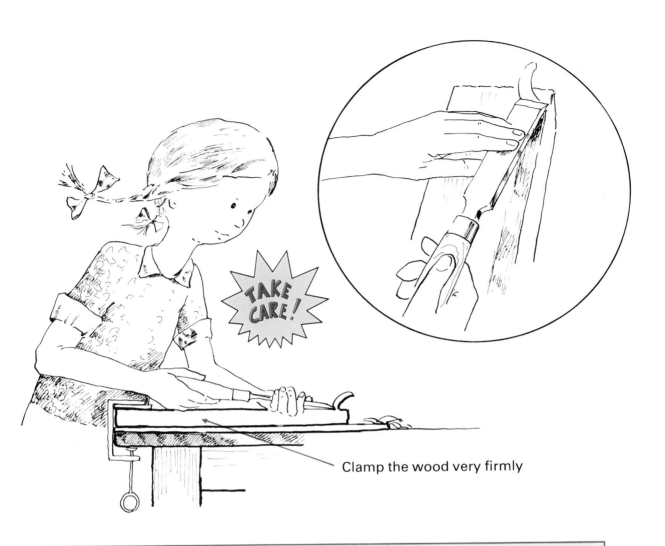

TAKE CARE!

Clamp the wood very firmly

Paring with a Chisel

Clamp the wood firmly. Never push with your arms, but lean into the work keeping control of your balance. Always keep your hands behind the tip of the blade. The sharper the tool the less effort it is. Control a sharp chisel rather than struggle with a blunt one. But mind your hands!

Gouge

This is held like a chisel. Cut from deep to shallow. For hollowing, use a mallet. Hold it in your right hand, and hit the gouge handle which is gripped in your left hand. A comfortably sized (30mm [1¼in] diameter) round log is better than a big square carpenter's mallet.

With practice, chisels and gouges will remove wood faster than a plane. They are used for smoothing, trimming, bevelling and hollowing wood.

Sawing

The tenon saw

Look at the blade. The little teeth are bent or 'set' to each side of the blade. This gives the blade space to move as the cut deepens. It is quicker to cut across the grain of the wood than with it but, whichever way, it is going to be slow work. Don't grip the handle and thrash away until your knuckles turn white. Use gentle pressure, and concentrate on keeping the saw straight. Let the saw, and time, do the work for you. A tenon saw's teeth are so small it will never be a fast saw, however hard you push.

Holding a saw

Hold the saw lightly, with your first finger pointing along the handle. Start the saw cut with the tip of your left thumb resting against the side of the blade and pull the tool slowly towards you. Move the saw slowly and cautiously until the cut is well started. Then you can move your left hand away from the blade.

For deep cuts, start at a corner, and point the blade downwards, until the saw has started its own channel, then increase the pressure at the back of the blade, and bring the saw slowly level.

Making a neat saw cut

It is very difficult to make a clean cut across the grain, as the first strokes of the saw tear the wood, leaving a ragged edge. So, mark the cutting line with a knife (**1**), and lightly chisel away the wood on the waste side of the line (**2**). Remember to keep your hands behind the blade. Lodge the saw in this groove, right against the line, and start sawing, initially steadying the saw with the left thumb as before (**3**).

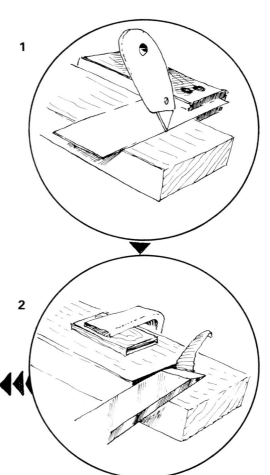

1

2

3

Planing

This is a shoulder plane. It is light, and can be used to cut across the end of a piece of timber as well as along the grain. The knurled wheel raises and lowers the blade, and the lever changes its angle. Never let your fingers curl underneath when you are lifting it, instead, lift it by its sides. Plane blades have to be very sharp. Prolong the life of the blade by lifting the tool off the wood on its return stroke, and by storing the plane on its side. If planing is really hard work, and you know the blade is sharp, rub a wax candle on its sole – this makes it much easier to push.

The plane is held as illustrated below.
1. Push the tool away from you, keeping hands and wrists clear of the wood to avoid splinters.

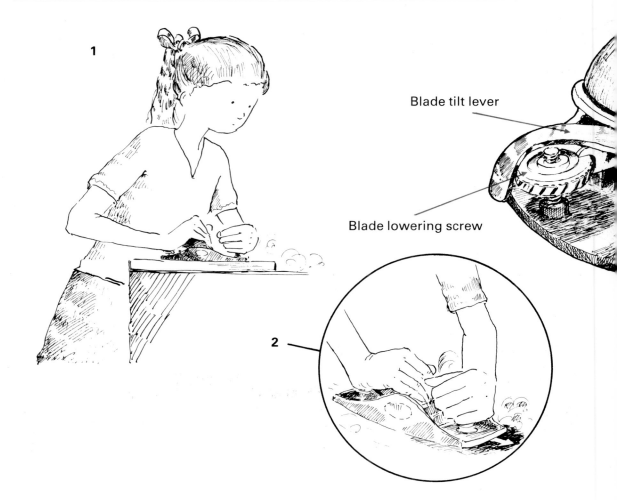

1

Blade tilt lever

Blade lowering screw

2

Dismantling the plane

Loosen clip 'A' and and remove
the cap iron 'B', then lift out blade.

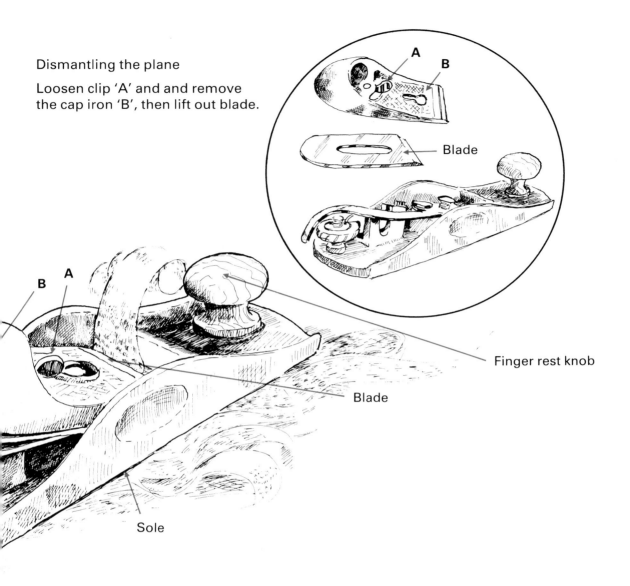

A B

Blade

Finger rest knob

Blade

B A

Sole

2. Plane in the direction of the grain, adjusting the plane so that it makes a fine cut, and removes lace-thin curly shavings. If the wood crackles and the shavings are coarse and broken up, try planing in the opposite direction, and winding the blade back a bit.
For sharpening advice see page 41.

Marking out

Measuring and marking out ought to be accurate. It is much easier and quicker to check and alter a line than to trim a saw cut in order to correct a mistake.

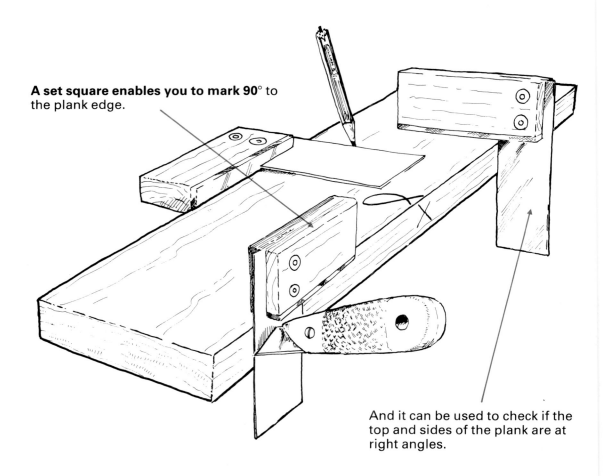

A set square enables you to mark 90° to the plank edge.

And it can be used to check if the top and sides of the plank are at right angles.

A set square provides a right angle and is used as illustrated above. Once an edge is straight, it can be used as a reference for other lines and measurements. A straight edge is identified with a pencil drawn loop, which starts and finishes at the straight edge. If the other face of the same edge is true and square, it is marked with a cross.

Clamping and Holding Wood

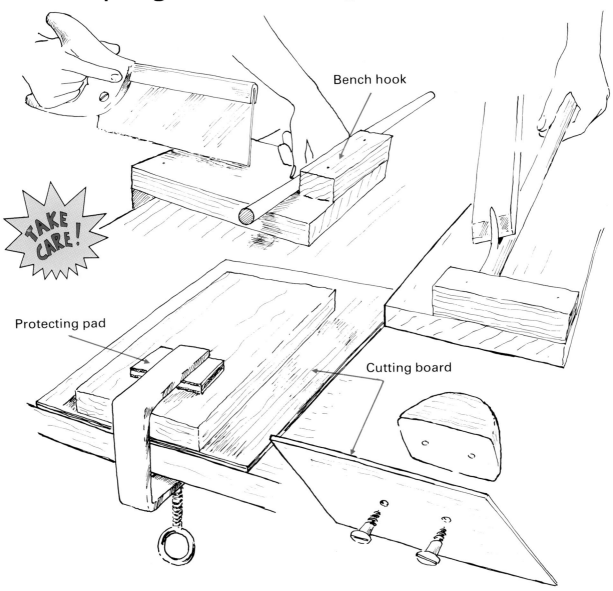

Bench hook

TAKE CARE!

Protecting pad

Cutting board

Woodworking is not hard work as long as the piece of wood you are shaping is held firmly. Wherever possible, use a clamp or a bench hook to hold the work. A bench hook is illustrated above. Hook it on to the edge of the bench to provide a firm block to press against when sawing or chiselling. If it is impossible to clamp the wood on to the table, screw some thin plywood to the underside of the wood, and then clamp the plywood. The piece can be unscrewed after it is shaped.

Wood

After a tree is felled and sawn into planks, the timber yard will leave the wood to dry. This can take several years, during which time the timber becomes lighter and harder.

Wood from the outer parts of a trunk contains more moisture than wood from the centre of the trunk, and it will shrink more. If you look at the grain pattern at the end of the plank, you can tell from which part of the tree trunk a plank was cut. Don't use fresh cut timber. Buy dry wood, and bring it into the house a few days before making any of these projects. Wood with a diagonal or short grain pattern will be very weak. Where the grain looks like this, it can snap suddenly and easily.

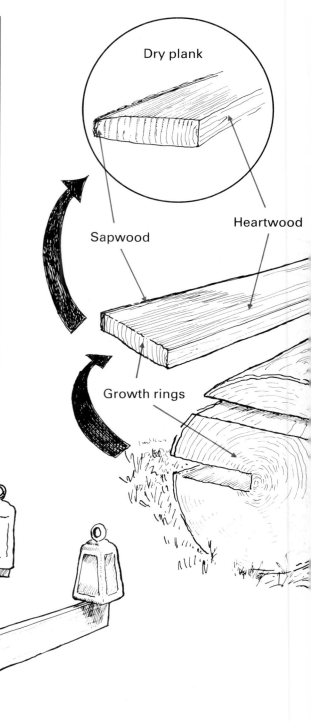

Dry plank

Sapwood

Heartwood

Growth rings

Used this way the wood will be strong and springy.

But used like this it will be much stronger and very rigid.

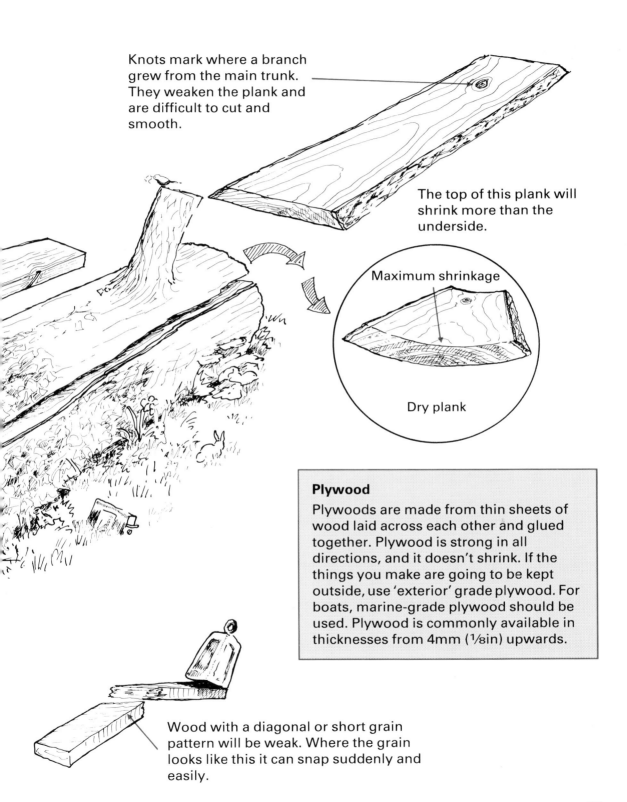

Knots mark where a branch grew from the main trunk. They weaken the plank and are difficult to cut and smooth.

The top of this plank will shrink more than the underside.

Maximum shrinkage

Dry plank

Plywood

Plywoods are made from thin sheets of wood laid across each other and glued together. Plywood is strong in all directions, and it doesn't shrink. If the things you make are going to be kept outside, use 'exterior' grade plywood. For boats, marine-grade plywood should be used. Plywood is commonly available in thicknesses from 4mm (1/8in) upwards.

Wood with a diagonal or short grain pattern will be weak. Where the grain looks like this it can snap suddenly and easily.

17

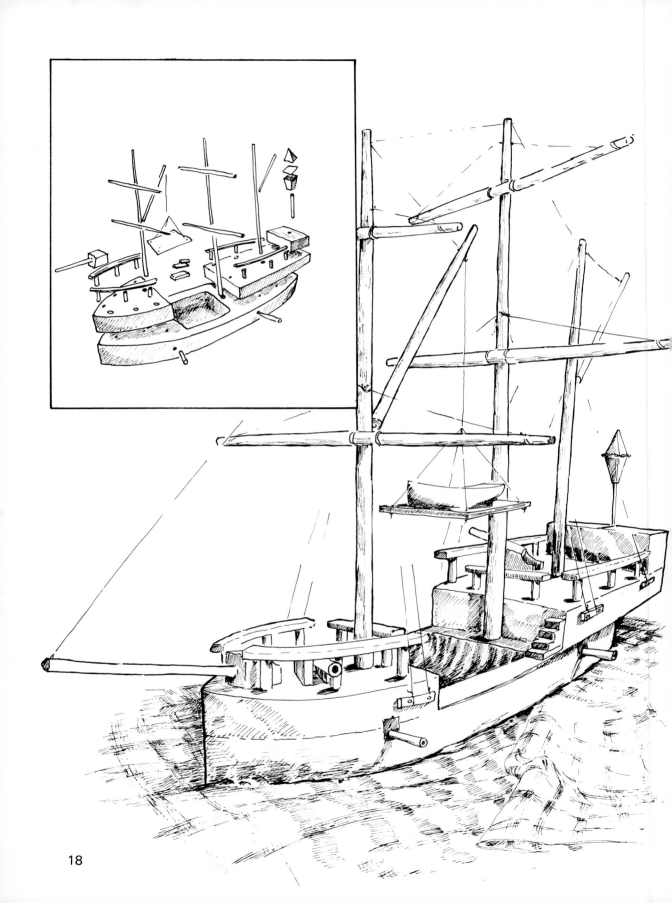

SHIPS AND GALLEONS

Tools: Tenon saw, chisel, mallet, gouge, sandpaper, fretsaw, drill, 6mm and 12mm drill bits, knife, hammer, adhesive tape, plane, pliers.

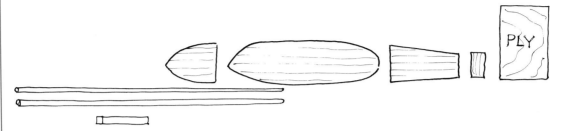

Materials: Veneer pins, cardboard, several clamps, spare wooden blocks, glue, thread, gimp pins, paint, varnish.

Not all the features on this ship are explained here – how about experimenting yourself to see what you can add?

Marking the Shape

1. Use a cardboard shape, called a template, to draw the galleon's outline on to your piece of wood. Your boat will be symmetrical if you use the same template for both sides, marking from the centre line. The same template is used again for the foredeck and poop. Use any shape you like for your template as long as it fits the wood.

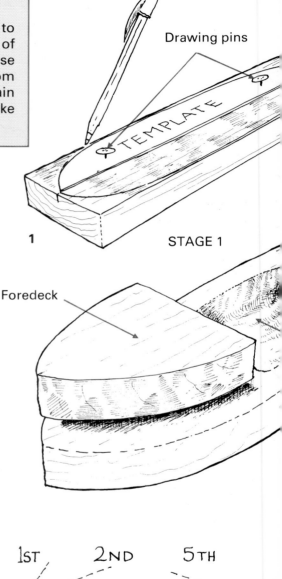

Drawing pins

TEMPLATE

1

STAGE 1

Foredeck

TAKE CARE!

2

Cutting the bow and stern

The three main pieces forming the body of the boat illustrated above are sawn separately. **2** and **3**. Clamp each piece tightly, with a board underneath it to protect the table, and follow **3** for the sequence of cuts to be made. Turn the wood around after sawing the bow and before sawing the stern. Finish all the saw cuts and then chop to the line with a chisel. Keep your hands behind the blade's tip.

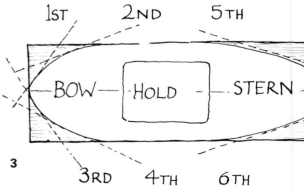

1ST   2ND   5TH

BOW — HOLD — STERN

3   3RD   4TH   6TH

20

Hollowing the hold

This is done with a mallet and a gouge, cutting along the grain. **4.** Mark the area to be hollowed out on to the main deck. Clamp the deck, pick up the mallet, then the gouge. Starting with cut A, gouge along and into the grain, 5mm (³/₁₆in) in from your line. Do not cut too far along the grain as the wood will already be splitting ahead of your gouge.

Poop

Hold

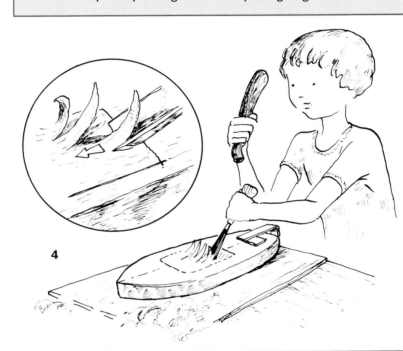

4

A second layer of cuts should follow beneath the first layer. Follow the drawings below which show the steps in hollowing the hold, viewed as though the hull had been sawn down the middle and you were looking into the sides of it.

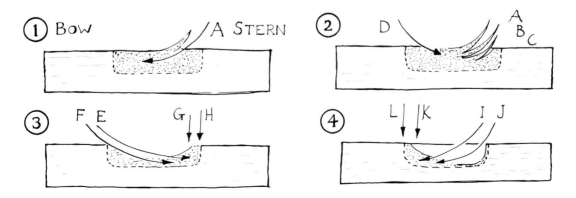

① Bow   A STERN

② D   A B C

③ F E   G H

④ L K   I J

Now that the hold is scooped out – it doesn't need to be really smooth, but sandpaper out the splinters – what about shaping the bottom and bows to make the boat more streamlined? Use the gouge, keeping both hands behind the tip of the blade.

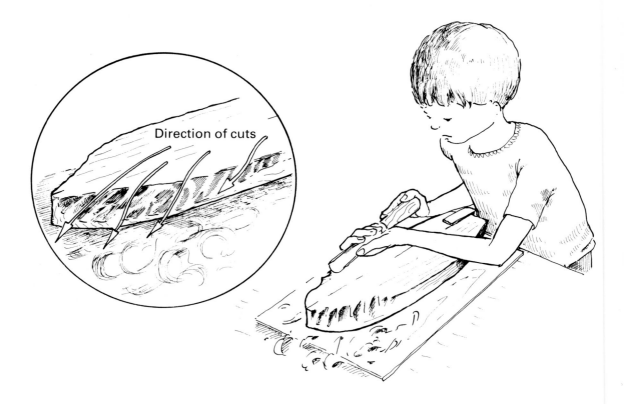

Direction of cuts

Always work lightly. If you have to push hard it is because:

● You are trying to cut off too much in one go.
● The gouge is blunt.
● You are cutting into, not out of the wood.

You can remove the worst ridges between the gouge marks with a chisel after you have finished gouging.
Now you can glue the boat together.

Glueing Wood

Preparation

- Collect enough clamps and wooden blocks to hold the galleon together. (The wooden blocks are to protect the decks from damage caused by the steel jaws.)
- Rough the surfaces to be glued together by scratching them with the blade of a tenon saw.
- Stack the pieces together, to see if you have enough clamps.

Warning

Until it is dry, woodworkers' glue is really slippery, and as your clamps tighten, the wood will slide out of position. To prevent this from happening:

Hammer three veneer pins into the hull beneath each deck, and cut them off just short of the wood, using pliers. These will provide the necessary grip – you can see them below. Tap the blocks into position and feel the difference, then separate again.

Now spread on the glue, and clamp up the job. Wipe away excess glue with a damp rag. Leave the boat for 12 hours in a warm room – but not too near a heater.

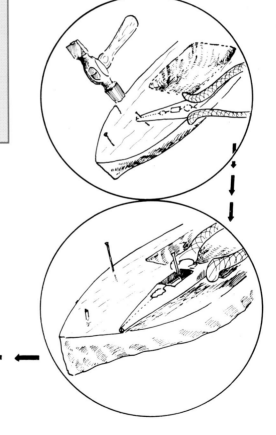

NOW GLUE IT

Drilling

Drilling holes for the masts

Holes for the masts have to be drilled on the deck centre line to a depth of about 15mm (⅝in). Clamp the boat to the table. Start with a 6mm (¼in) drill bit. From the front each mast should be upright and in line but from the side only the tallest mast should be upright, the others should lean. If you get the angles wrong, a bigger drill can correct them.

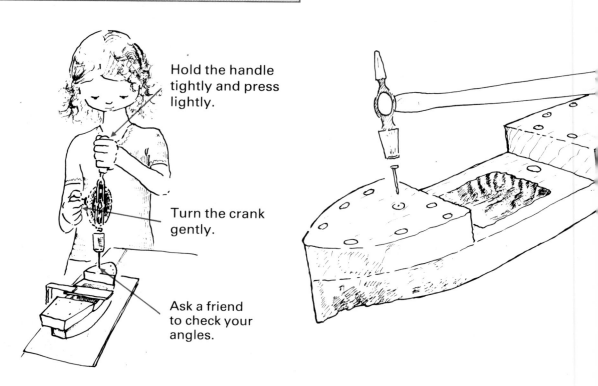

Hold the handle tightly and press lightly.

Turn the crank gently.

Ask a friend to check your angles.

Pull out the drill every 5mm (³⁄₁₆in), so that it doesn't stick. When the 6mm (¼in) holes are drilled, drop a 6mm (¼in) dowel into each one to check the angle. Now fit the 12mm (½in) drill bit, and bore out the holes, correcting the angles where necessary.

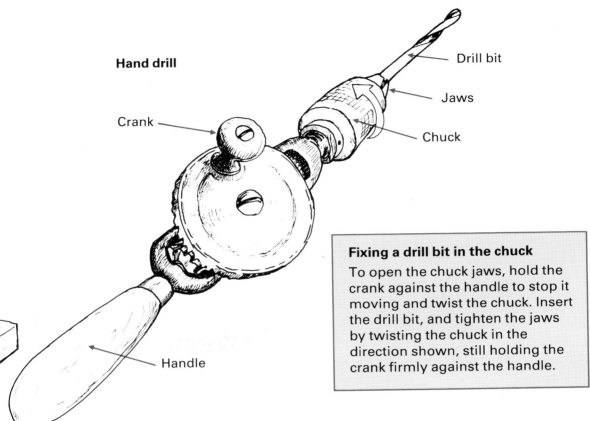

Hand drill

Drill bit

Jaws

Crank

Chuck

Handle

Fixing a drill bit in the chuck

To open the chuck jaws, hold the crank against the handle to stop it moving and twist the chuck. Insert the drill bit, and tighten the jaws by twisting the chuck in the direction shown, still holding the crank firmly against the handle.

Drilling holes for the side posts

Mark and punch a centre point for each post using a hammer and nail as illustrated opposite. Make all the post holes about 8mm (5/16in) deep. To do this choose a suitable scrap of wood and drill right through it, so that only 8mm (5/16in) of drill pokes out underneath. Choose a suitable wood off-cut and drill through it. Small adjustments to drill length can be made by moving the drill further into the chuck.

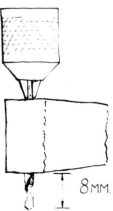

8MM.

Drill around the edges of the decks at each marked point, and then sandpaper the decks smooth. The galleon is now ready for the posts and handrails, guns and masts.

Cutting the dowels

The posts should be about 10mm (⅜in) high, so they need to be 18mm (¾in) long.

Mark the posts on the side of the 6mm (¼in) dowel. Use a knife and roll the blade over each mark to weaken the dowel and prepare it for sawing. Place the dowel on the bench hook and saw the posts off, rotating the dowel slowly as the saw cuts through. Don't press hard or the dowel will splinter.

The masts should be cut from 12mm (½in) dowels. The main mast should be a little bit longer than the boat and each mast should get thinner at the top. So, after cutting them, rest each one on the table. Hold the bottom of the mast in the left hand and slide the plane to its tip. Turn the mast around a little, and do it again. Repeat round the mast several times, cutting away the resulting ridges with the plane as you go.

Glueing the posts and masts

Before glueing in the masts drill them for the pulleys – skip to page 29. After fitting the pulleys you can glue the masts. Squirt a little glue into each hole. The dowels will draw the glue in with them. Before tapping in the posts and masts, take each one in turn. Hold it against the bench hook and chisel a groove or shaving from its side. This will allow air and excess glue to escape when the post is hammered in. Remember to keep both hands behind the blade when you use the chisel.

TAKE CARE!

Trimming the posts

Some of the dowels will have to be trimmed, but wait until the glue is dry. Then, take a scrap of wood 10mm (³⁄₈in) thick (the height of the posts), and about 150mm (6in) long, and drill a 6mm (¹⁄₄in) hole in it. Work the drill in and out of the hold to enlarge it. Then slip it over each dowel. Posts that are much too long can be cut back with the saw resting on the wood. Those that are slightly too long can be trimmed with a chisel. Keep your hands behind the chisel blade.

Fitting the handrails

These are made from plywood. The curved ones are cut with a fretsaw (for advice on using a fretsaw see pages 35 and 36). Cut the plywood to the required lengths (see instructions on page 34) and round the edges by rubbing them against sandpaper laid on the table. Place them over the posts and mark the position for each nail with a pencil.

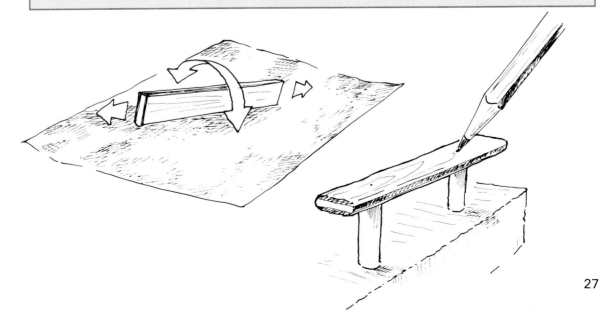

Nailing on the handrails

The handrails should be drilled before they are nailed to the posts. You won't have a drill bit of the right size for this, so take a veneer pin, cut off its head, and fit the pin in the chuck of the hand drill. It may be necessary to wrap some adhesive tape around the end of the pin to help the jaws grip.

Clamp the handrail, and drill the holes where marked. Don't press, or the cheap drill bit will bend.

Spot glue on the end of each post. Fit a nail in each hole on the handrail, position the handrail, and hammer the nails into the posts.

The cannons

These are made from two small pieces of ply and a dowel. They are held by a single veneer pin which also allows the barrel to swing up and down.

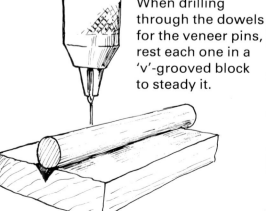

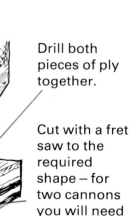

Drill both pieces of ply together.

Cut with a fret saw to the required shape – for two cannons you will need four trolley sides.

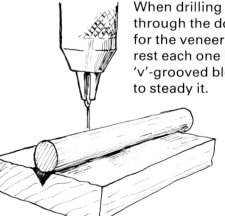

When drilling through the dowels for the veneer pins, rest each one in a 'v'-grooved block to steady it.

Stern Lantern

This is quite a big lantern. It is made from a length of 12mm (½in) square pine. Press its end against the bench hook and chisel it to a point. Keep both hands behind the tip of the blade. Saw off the point, about 12-14mm (½-⅝in) from the end (piece **1**).

TAKE CARE!

1

2

For piece **2**, drill a hole in the end of the remaining piece of wood, big enough for a matchstick or a toothpick. Then use the chisel to taper the wood, remembering to mind your hands. Saw this piece off, too. Cut a square of card or plywood for the rim, and glue all the pieces together on to a matchstick pole.

Pulleys

Use a veneer pin to make each pulley. Bend it around the end of some pliers. Then drill a hole in the mast and glue the pulley into the hole.

Rigging

Bent veneer pins

Thread

Spot glue on to the knots.
Use either of these knots.

Plywood

Gimp pins

Main rigging threads

Painting

For a sea-going boat
1. Smooth each part with 220 grit sandpaper, pressed against a foam pad.
2. Paint the hull and decks and posts with household undercoat white paint.
3. Sand the boat lightly.
4. Apply the topcoat. Work downwards, using one colour at a time, painting the posts, guns, decks, etc. Start the next colour when the previous coats are absolutely dry. Household gloss paints are suitable, but the modelmakers' oil gloss paints provide a better variety of colours.
5. Use varnish on masts and handrails, and perhaps those pieces painted with gold or silver paint, to make them glitter.

For a display boat
1. Use emulsion paint for the hull and decks. Apply it thinned with water, and sand the boat lightly after it has dried.
2. Paint another coat, making it thicker in some places than in others. Let the brush strokes move from the front to the back to give the effect of planking.
3. Complete detail with gloss paints as described above.
4. Varnish handrails, masts and yards, and any silver and gold work.

Cleaning up

Clean your brushes immediately after finishing with each colour and before starting the next. Emulsion paint is removed with warm water and washing-up liquid. Pour a little washing-up liquid in the palm of your hand and gently dab and wipe the brush in the palm. Use more fresh soap, and then rinse the brush by holding it under warm tap water, stroking the brush hairs until they are clean.

Oil paints are removed with white spirit. Pour a little into a small glass jar, and prod the brush into the bottom. When most of the paint has been removed, finish with soap and water. Dry before use.

DOLLS' HOUSE

Tools: Tenon saw, plane, fretsaw, 'V' supports, drill, file, hammer, set square, ruler.
Materials: Veneer pins, gimp pins, calico, glue, paint.

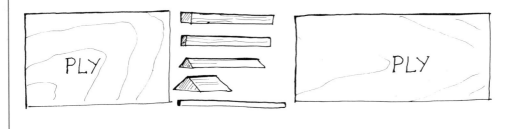

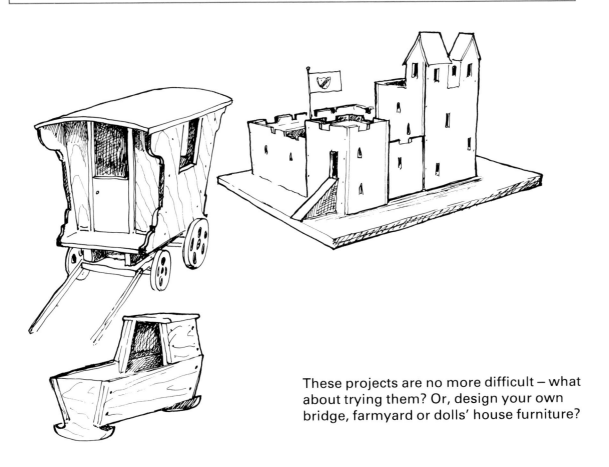

These projects are no more difficult – what about trying them? Or, design your own bridge, farmyard or dolls' house furniture?

Sawing Plywood

If you don't know how to saw plywood, it can be really difficult because the saw jams.

This is how to do it: Clamp the wood to the edge of the table, with the piece that has to be cut off overhanging the edge. Then saw lightly, only cutting with the push stroke. As soon as the saw is about 75mm (3in) along the line and sawing is becoming a struggle, bend the waste downwards with your left hand. This stops it jamming the saw.

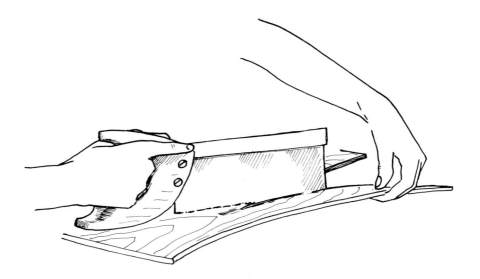

Planing a Plywood Edge

The corners are very easy to damage. Don't worry. To limit the damage, plane the cross grain edges first, and then down the sides of the board. Or plane inwards from the edges.

Fretsawing

The fretsaw is very fragile. It cuts curves and corners in thin wood and only cuts on the down stroke. Its teeth are so small that you have to feel the blade to find out which way up to fit it.

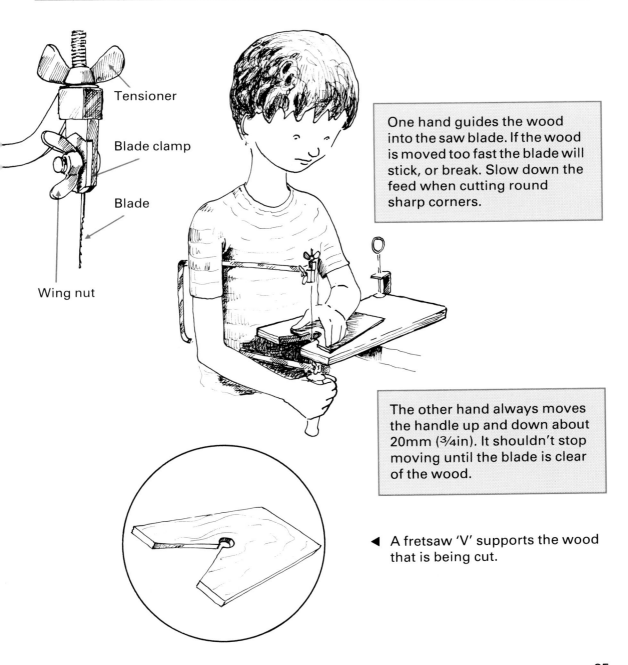

Tensioner

Blade clamp

Blade

Wing nut

One hand guides the wood into the saw blade. If the wood is moved too fast the blade will stick, or break. Slow down the feed when cutting round sharp corners.

The other hand always moves the handle up and down about 20mm (3/4in). It shouldn't stop moving until the blade is clear of the wood.

◀ A fretsaw 'V' supports the wood that is being cut.

Fretsawing windows and doors

Mark these out with a sharp knife and a straightedge. The fretsaw will tend to follow the knife cut. Drill a hole through each window and the balcony door, so that the blade can be slipped through. Unscrew the tensioner and wing nut clamping the blade and feed the blade through the hole. Re-clamp it. Tighten the tension screw. Ask for help with this; it is a three-handed job. Now cut across to the knife cut, and follow it around the window, slowing or stopping the feed at each corner. Always keep the saw blade moving. Release the blade and level the cuts with a file if necessary.

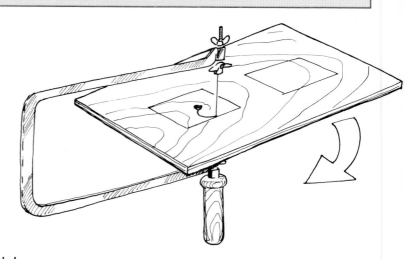

Cutting decorative boards

One saw cut gives two boards! Always draw the outline on to the plywood first.

Cutting balcony supports

Cut the balcony supports from a long strip, sawing off the finished work before continuing to cut the next. This makes the work easier to hold.

Assembling the Exterior

The house is put together with gimp pins and glue.

First stage

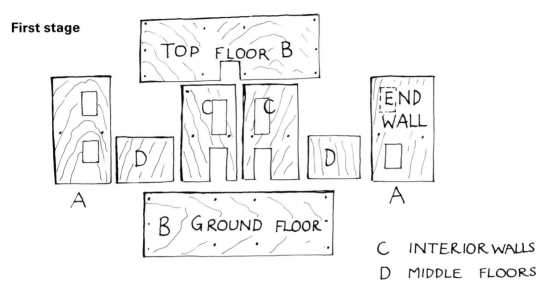

Mark out interior floor and wall positions.
Drill the nail holes as shown.

C   INTERIOR WALLS
D   MIDDLE FLOORS

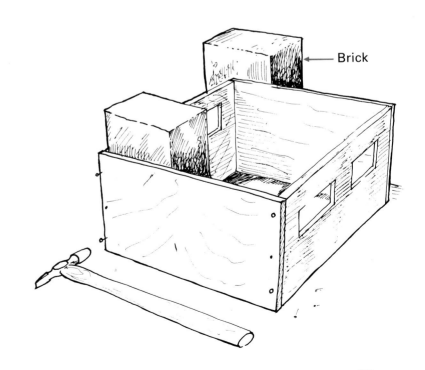

Brick

Second stage

Nail the end walls (**A**) and ground and top floors (**B**) together, after glueing their edges. Bricks help hold the sides and absorb the shock of the hammer blows. (If you don't use bricks, the sides nailed first shake apart as the second are being hammered together.)

Assembling the Interior

Floors and Walls

Nail the edges of the mid-floors (**D**) to the middle of the interior walls (**C**), and insert and nail them in place in the house.

Doors

Cut each door from a piece of plywood. Make a hinge as illustrated using a strip of calico. Let the glue dry thoroughly before trying the door out.

Stairs

There are two flights of stairs. Each flight is made up as illustrated opposite and glued to a plywood board. Put a pad and a weight onto them while the glue sets, to hold them in place.

The stair rails must be fitted before the stairs are installed. The pillars support the landing floor and are glued to the interior walls. A bent postcard will hold these pillars against the walls while the glue dries.

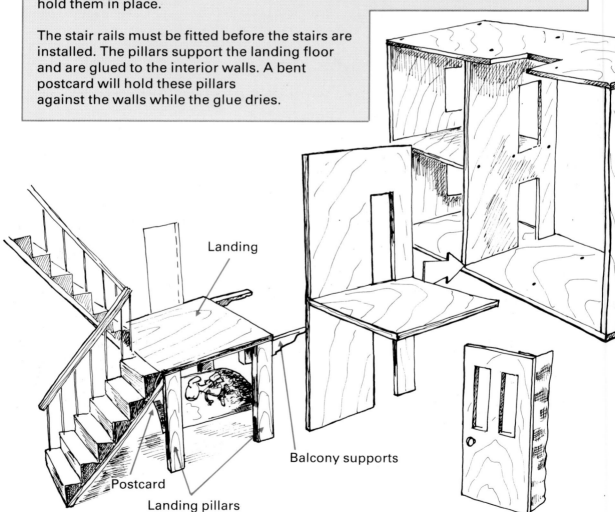

Landing

Balcony supports

Postcard

Landing pillars

Balcony support holes. Mark and cut them to allow the support to glue against the inner walls or landing pillers.

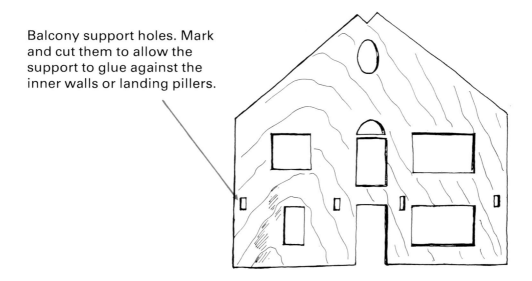

Assembling the stairs and balcony

Make the rails from strips of plywood with the edges rounded using sandpaper. Fit them using veneer pins as uprights – their heads should be cut off first. For the stairs, each pin is fixed into a hole drilled into each step and the top poked through the base of the handrail. Before assembling the balcony, drill holes in both the top and bottom rails simultaneously. Drill through the bottom rail first and remember not to drill completely through the top rail. Glue the bottom rail to the edge of the balcony base. Reinforce each post with a drop of glue at its end and make sure the uprights are vertical before leaving to dry.

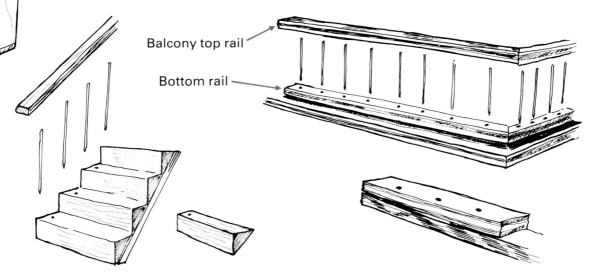

Balcony top rail

Bottom rail

Attaching the roof

Nail on the roof after all the interior work is finished. Both roof pieces of plywood are nailed to a square ridge beam before being nailed to the walls. Cut a board to fit over the back of the house to keep its contents clean and safe when the house isn't being lived in.

Dormer window

This is a really simple dormer window. The roof is made from a triangular section of pine. Two small pieces of plywood fit beneath and are shaped to slot into the main roof of the doll's house. The decorative barge boards are drilled and tacked on with gimp pins before the complete dormer is glued in place.

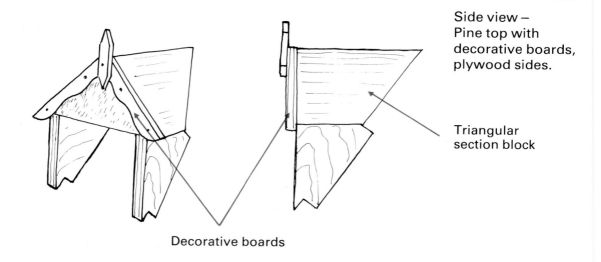

Side view –
Pine top with decorative boards, plywood sides.

Triangular section block

Decorative boards

Painting

Household paints are quite suitable, but try finding samples of wallpaper fabric and flooring material that could be used inside and outside the house to add variety to the textures and colours. Model shops sell books of dolls' house wallpaper. Finish all the paintwork before wallpapering and laying the floor coverings.

Now look at the galleon and the lorry. With the methods and tricks used there, why not make some furniture for the house?

Sharpening

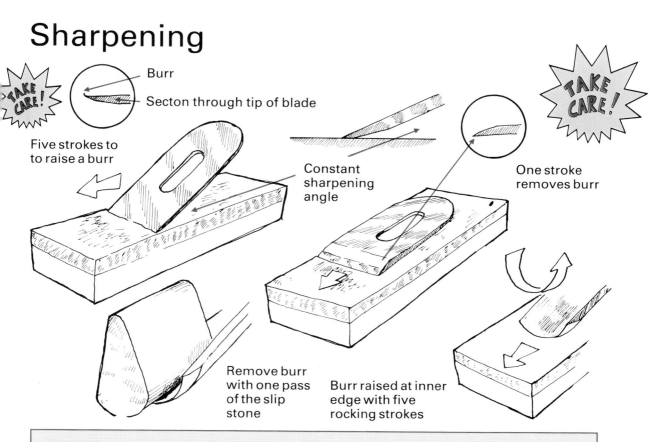

Burr

Secton through tip of blade

TAKE CARE!

TAKE CARE!

Five strokes to to raise a burr

Constant sharpening angle

One stroke removes burr

Remove burr with one pass of the slip stone

Burr raised at inner edge with five rocking strokes

Planes, knives, chisels and gouges should be as sharp as razors. They are easier to use, and need much less force to push them into the wood when they are sharp. But sharpening tools is quite difficult, so you should ask your parents or your teacher to help. You will need some lubrication oil, a medium oilstone and a fine oilstone. The important points to remember are:

- Oil the sharpening stones
- Keep the tool at a constant angle
- Reduce tool pressure after the first burr has been raised
- Change to a smoother stone after the burr has been raised and removed twice
- Grind the edges on the stone in the proportion of 5:1; that is, five times on the bevel side, one time on the flat
- Don't drop the tools, bang them together, or run the tools into nails, etc. Look after the edge once it is sharp.

Gouges have to be sharpened with a curved slip stone. Grind the gouge along the sharpening stone until a roughness can be felt when you slide your hand lightly up the inside of the blade.

Oil the slip stone and slide it up and down inside the blade to remove the roughness. Repeat with the fine oilstone and with the slip stone several times. Be careful not to vary the sharpening angle, and please mind your hands.

Sequence for assembly

Chassis beams (**A**) to chassis top (**B**)
Engine bonnet (**C**) to deck (**D**)
Cabin (**E**) to deck (**D**)
Deck (**D**) to chassis top (**B**)

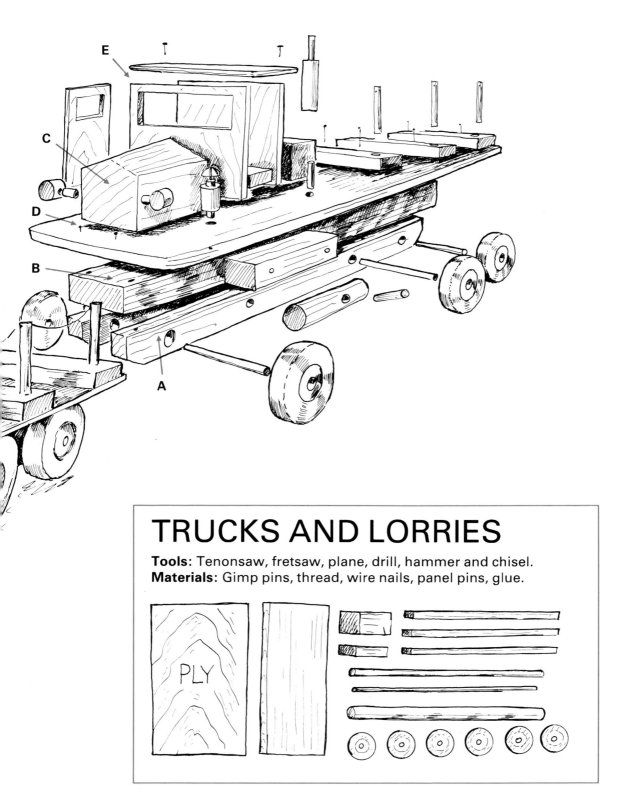

TRUCKS AND LORRIES

Tools: Tenonsaw, fretsaw, plane, drill, hammer and chisel.
Materials: Gimp pins, thread, wire nails, panel pins, glue.

PLY

Truck building

Clamp the two chassis beams together, and mark the positions for the axles on both sides. Punch the centres, and drill them.

Start drilling on one side using a 6mm (¼in) drill bit and stop halfway. Turn the chassis over, and drill right through from the other side. Continue to wind the drill in the hole once it is through so the axles are a loose fit and turn easily.

The axles are cut from the 6mm (¼in) dowel. Cut them to length, and push them into the axle holes. Position the beams about 40mm (1⅝in) apart, and apply glue to the tops of the beams.

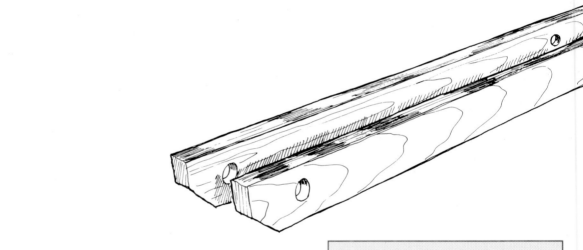

Place the wooden chassis top over them, and clamp it down. Then, lining up the top with the ends of the beams, hammer a panel pin through the chassis top, into one chassis beam's end. Fix the other beam to the chassis top in the same way and continue driving in the panel pins at intervals of about 75mm (3ins).

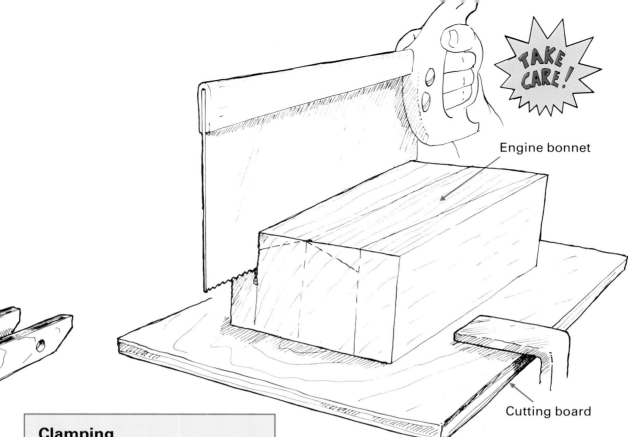

TAKE CARE!

Engine bonnet

Cutting board

Clamping

The bonnet is a difficult shape to clamp, and will become more and more difficult as you complete the shaping. To help you, and before starting work on it, screw the bonnet block to the cutting board, and then clamp the cutting board to the table.

This trick of screwing the piece on to the cutting board before you work on it comes in very useful, and it is nearly always worth the little extra effort required. It means you have the piece you are working on safe, firm, and uncluttered by metal clamps.

Begin shaping by sawing the taper for the bonnet, then chisel and plane the top slopes. Keep your hands behind the blade. When the top shaping is finished, unscrew the bonnet, and sand the sides to remove saw marks.

Order for assembly

1. Nail and glue **C** to **D**.
2. Nail and glue **E** to **C**.
3. Nail and glue **F** to **D**.
4. Nail and glue **G** to **H**.
5. Nail and glue **G** to **F** and **H** to **D**.

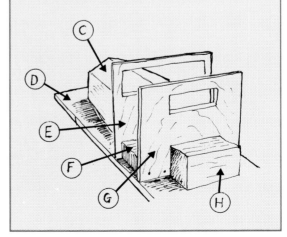

Nailing

Nailing may seem quick and easy, but you will need to know a few tricks and practise a little before you can work quickly, without bending the nails, splitting the wood or mashing your fingers.

Nails should be about 2½ to 3 times the thickness of the piece being fixed.

Hold the hammer as illustrated, with your first finger straight along the handle. Use your wrist rather than the forearm for the hammering action, unless you are using a heavy hammer. For the nails described in this book, you want a light pin hammer. Big hammers are for big nails. When hammering, keep your wrist low down, close to the wood, and make sure that the hammer face is clean and dry.

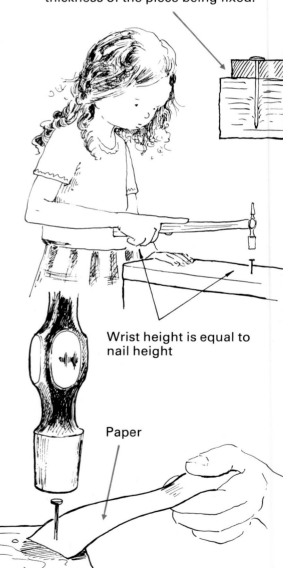

Wrist height is equal to nail height

Paper

Starting a small nail

If the nail is too small to hold, or is in an awkward position, cut a strip of paper and poke the nail through its end. Then, hold the paper and position the nail. Hammer the nail into the wood. Tear away the paper after the nail is started.

Pulling out bent nails

As soon as the nail begins to bend, stop and pull it out; it is difficult to remove bent nails buried deep in the wood. Use pliers or nail pullers, called pincers, to pull out the nails, and slip a block of wood under the tool to protect the wood surface.

Pincers

Pliers

Gimp pin: Usually painted black, but available in other colours. Has a flat head, and is excellent for toymaking.

Veneer pin: Very thin, wire nail, ideal for holding work while glue dries. Useful for hinges, pulleys, etc. Panel pins are similar but thicker.

Wire nail: Flat-headed and used for general work, but heads are ugly and difficult to hide. Pre-drilling often necessary.

Difficulties in nailing

If the nails don't hold the wood together:
- Support the pieces you are hammering together – put a brick or something solid and heavy underneath the piece you are nailing.
- The nails might be too short, find some longer ones.
- If the piece being fixed is curved, one nail might rock the other out. Straighten the curve.
- Drill a pilot hole.

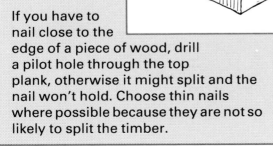

If you have to nail close to the edge of a piece of wood, drill a pilot hole through the top plank, otherwise it might split and the nail won't hold. Choose thin nails where possible because they are not so likely to split the timber.

Dowels

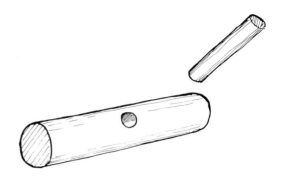

Fuel tanks

These are made of lengths of 12mm (½in) and 6mm (¼in) dowels. The latter holds the tank in place, and is left as the filler cap (illustrated below).

Chassis (**A**)

Wire

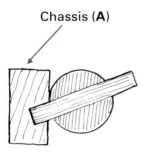

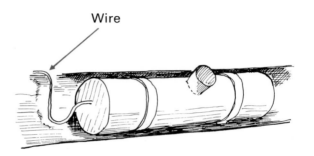

Silencer

Drill the end of a piece of 12mm (½in) dowel first with a 3mm (⅛in) drill bit, then with a 6mm (¼in) drill bit. The small drill bit will help begin the hole which is often quite difficult to achieve in the end grain. Hold the dowel in a groove using the clamp as illustrated.

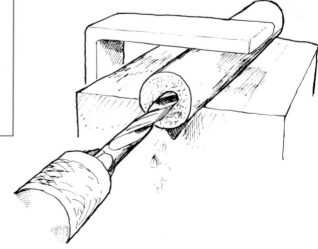

The outside of this pretty house was painted with emulsion paint, then decorated inside and out with bright watercolour paints (fixed with a spray lacquer for cars). The curtains are sewn around toothpicks Sellotaped together and wedged into the corners.

To make the boxes look rich, use a good stain and coloured varnish. Scrape the brasswork clean with a penknife when the varnish is dry.

The stools have matchsticks legs pushed into holes drilled into the seat. (Mark and drill the holes before cutting out the seat.) The table legs are glued into notches cut into the corners of a triangular piece of plywood under the round top. The settle is plywood, glued and pinned together. The effect of planking is achieved by making vertical saw-cuts on both sides of the back, which also enables the wood to be bent easily around the curved back of the seat.

The contrasts of bright yellow and silver paint against the dark hull give this galleon a very powerful appearance.

The car running board and mudguards are each made from a strip of pine, which is bent by soaking it in boiling water for ten minutes. This makes it pliable and so easier to bend into shape. You must wear thick rubber gloves and an apron when doing this because the wood has to be bent while it is really hot. Once bent and allowed to cool it will keep its shape. The front seat is hinged with pins (like the lorry door), and can be pushed forward to let Badger get out.

The battleship cabins are made from plywood and blocks, nailed with gimp pins. The gun turrets are pivoted on dowels which stick up through the deck. Railings are panel pins, with thread tied between them. The bamboo funnels are glued over dowels which poke up at an angle through the main deck. Portholes are drilled into the cabins.

Door Hinges

Why not make the doors open and shut? Fit them as though they were going to be nailed inside the door frame. Looking from above, the cabin door will look like the illustration below.

Mark in the pivot points in the top of the roof and the floor of the cabin. They should be the same distance in from the framework of the door.

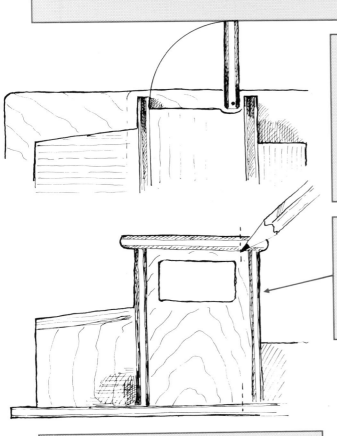

Drill the top pivot using a veneer pin in the hand drill (see page 28 for advice), and because drilling downwards will be difficult, hammer another pin a little way down through the floor of the cabin to mark the lower pivot. Wiggle this one about with a pair of pliers before pulling it out.

Next, put the door in place and draw on to the door the position of the two holes. Then drill these in the top and bottom of the door, with the door clamped to the edge of the table.

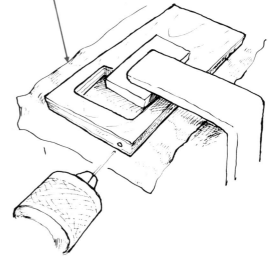

Tap a pin into the bottom of the door, and cut off its head, leaving about 3mm (1/8in) showing. Insert the door, feeding the bottom pivot into the nail hole. Drop a pin down through the roof into the door. Don't hammer this in until after the truck is painted – painting is best done with the moveable parts removed.

49

Cattle Truck or Horse Box

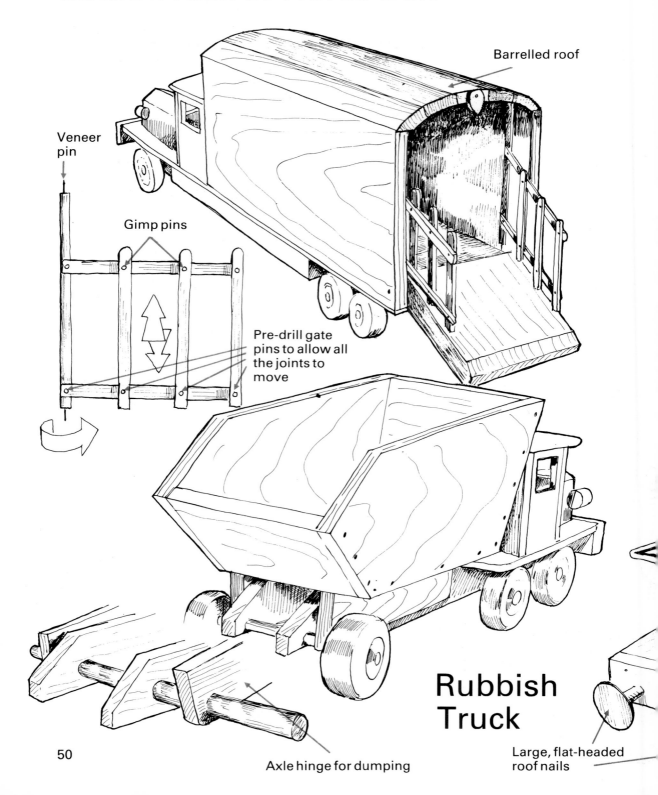

Barrelled roof

Veneer pin

Gimp pins

Pre-drill gate pins to allow all the joints to move

Rubbish Truck

Axle hinge for dumping

Large, flat-headed roof nails

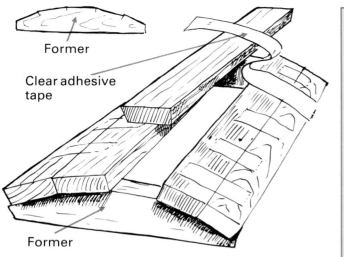

Former

Clear adhesive tape

Former

Tank Engine

Barrelling

1. Cut two formers (one to support each end) shaped to the inside curve of the roof.
2. Mark off the number of planks to be used.
3. Level off the areas between the marks.
4. Cover the formers with plastic film, so the planks don't stick to the formers.
5. Take two planks and plane one edge of the second plank to make it fit snugly.
6. Spread glue on the edge of the first plank, and slide the second against it. Bring the ends level, hold them together with adhesive tape.
7. When the glue is dry, add a new plank, remembering only to plane the touching edge of the piece being fitted.
8. Plane the roof round, before lifting it from the formers.

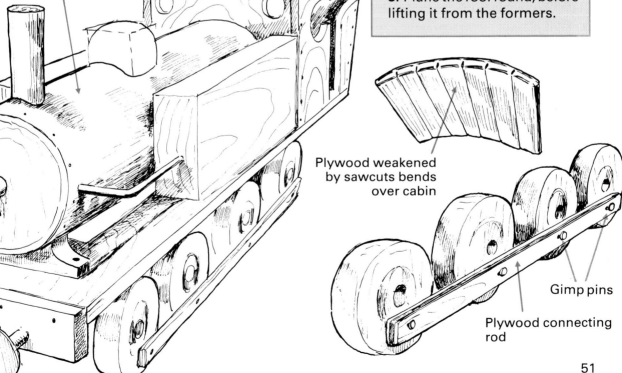

Plastic drain pipe

Plywood weakened by sawcuts bends over cabin

Gimp pins

Plywood connecting rod

BOXES

The top is glued to the edges of the side, and the joint is then strengthened with glued strips.

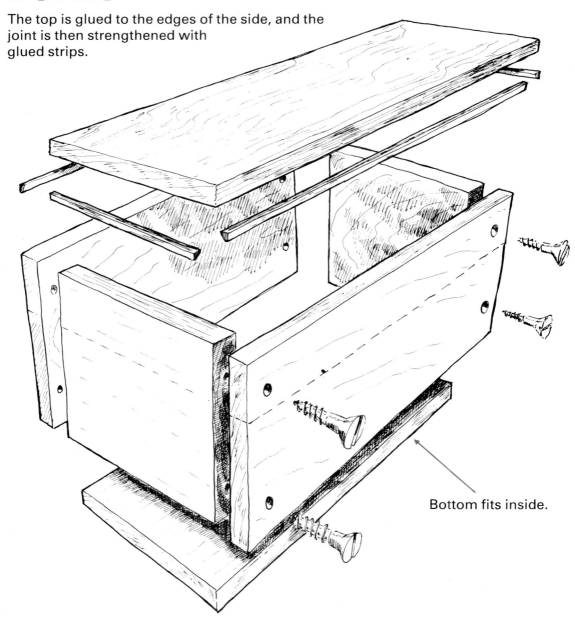

Bottom fits inside.

The clever thing is that you saw the top off once the box is finished, and it fits exactly!

Tools: Tenon saw, plane, drill, assorted drill bits, screwdriver, glue, string.

Materials: Screws, veneer pins, nails, strip of leather, wood.

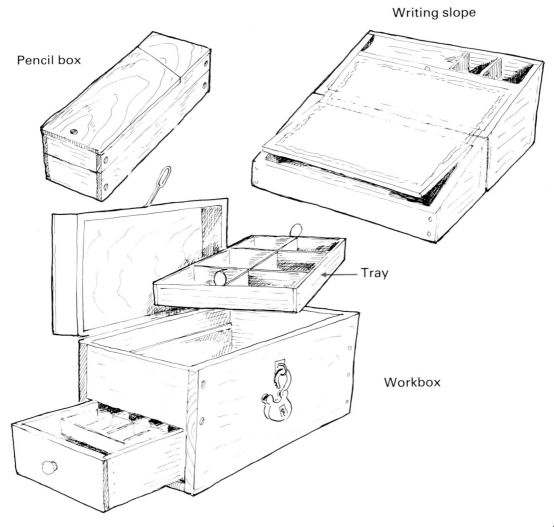

Writing slope

Pencil box

Tray

Workbox

Making Boxes

Boxes are not as easy to make as you might think. In order to look good they have to be neatly put together, with clean sharp edges, and smooth surfaces. Handle the wood cautiously, and remember that all the dents and scratches will have to be sandpapered out, which is quite hard work and takes ages. Better to look after the wood in the first place.

Box parts are usually in pairs. Cut and trim them in twos, so that they are identical in size.

Planing end-grain

The plane blade must be very sharp.

Stack the two pieces of wood together, and clamp them on to a shooting board, slightly overhanging the edge.

Rest the side of the shoulder plane on the table and slide the plane along the edge of the board. The plane will remove fine shavings from the end-grain of the pieces which overhang the board. The block at the end of the board should stop the wood splitting. If there are difficulties which cannot be overcome by using less blade and reducing the overhang, you will have to turn the plank and work inwards from both edges.

Using Screws

Roundhead

Countersink →

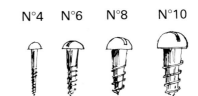

Countersunk bit ——→

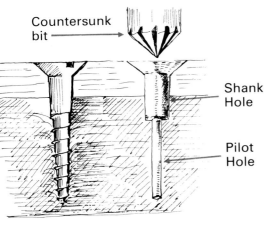

Shank Hole

Pilot Hole

Choosing the correct screw and screwdriver

Screws are sold in different lengths and thicknesses.

● There are several types of tops. The countersunk screws, especially brass ones, can be neat and decorative.

● The thicker the diameter of the screw, the greater its holding power, and the higher its number.

● Each screw requires two holes. The first is the pilot hole, which is about half the diameter of the screw spiral. The second is the shank hole which has to be the diameter of the cut shank. A large drill bit or a countersink bit can be used to sink the head level with the surface of the wood.

● Support the wood as if you were nailing it. When the screws are in, line up the screw slots so they are all pointing the same way (it's a mark of a neat craftsman).

● Use the right screwdriver. It must fit exactly into the slot: too thin, and it will damage the screw when it is tightening up. Too wide, and it will tear up the wood.

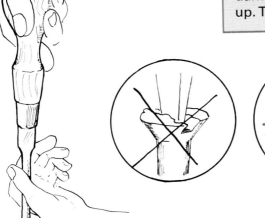

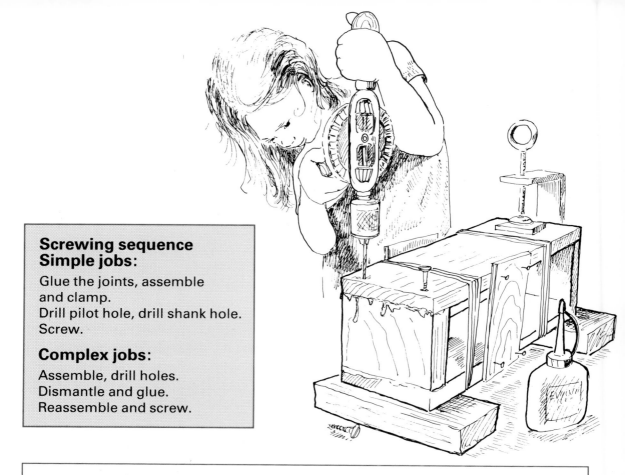

Screwing sequence
Simple jobs:

Glue the joints, assemble
and clamp.
Drill pilot hole, drill shank hole.
Screw.

Complex jobs:

Assemble, drill holes.
Dismantle and glue.
Reassemble and screw.

When the sides are screwed and the glue is dry, plane round the top edge and glue on the top. Hold down the top with weights until the glue dries. Trim the bottom plank, and glue it inside the bottom rim. Plane and sand the sides and corners, taking care at the corners not to split the wood. Always plane inwards, don't let the plane glide off the box or it might splinter the edges. Sandpaper the box smooth and flat before sawing off the lid.

Sawing off the lid

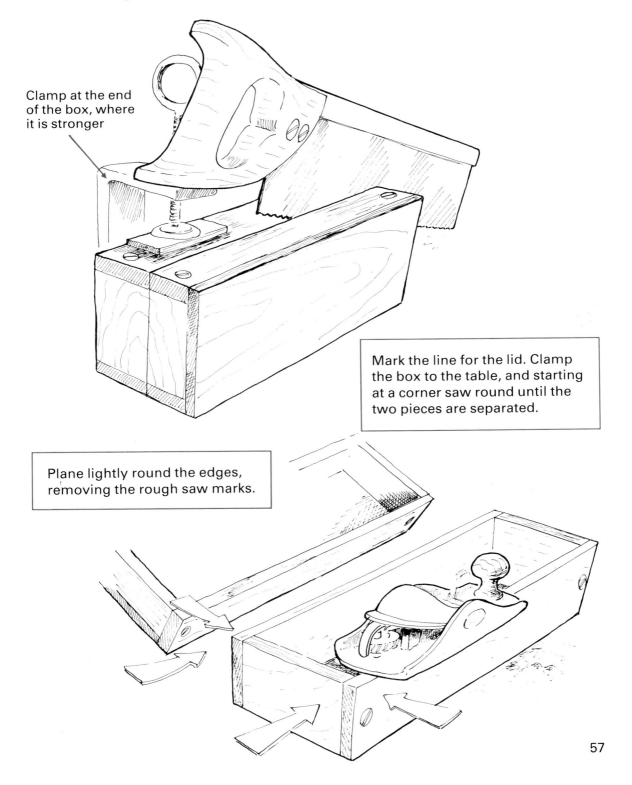

Clamp at the end of the box, where it is stronger

Mark the line for the lid. Clamp the box to the table, and starting at a corner saw round until the two pieces are separated.

Plane lightly round the edges, removing the rough saw marks.

Hinges

Fasten hinges with short countersunk screws.

1. Place the lid in position and clamp the box to the bench. Mark the hinge positions.

2. Open the hinge, and rest it on a block so that its pivot is exactly in line with the lid joint.

3. Drill and screw the hinge in place with countersunk screws.

4. Repeat for the second hinge.

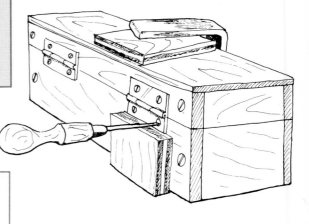

Drawers

Drawers are glued and nailed with veneer pins.

1. Choose an attractive piece of wood for the drawer front and cut it so that it fits exactly into place.

2. Cut the sides and back. These are narrower because the bottom of the drawer is nailed beneath the sides.

3. Cut an extra doubling piece to glue to the front.

Pre-drill the sides and base before nailing. Screw or nail and glue the doubling piece to the drawer front.

Handles

A small slip of leather makes a good handle for a drawer, as it will flap down when the drawer is not in use. Drill right through the centre of the drawer front, put some glue in the hole, and then poke in a thin strip of leather. Wedge a small pointed stick into the hole from inside the drawer, to hold the leather in place.

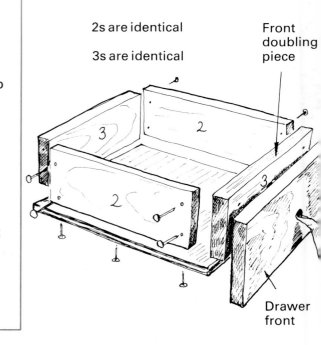

2s are identical

3s are identical

Front doubling piece

Drawer front

Trays

Trays are made like drawers, only there is no false front. They rest on small strips or battens nailed and glued inside the box.

Once the tray is made, fit divisions inside it. These are made from strips of wood, slightly higher than the sides. Round the top with the shoulder plane, smoothing with sandpaper.

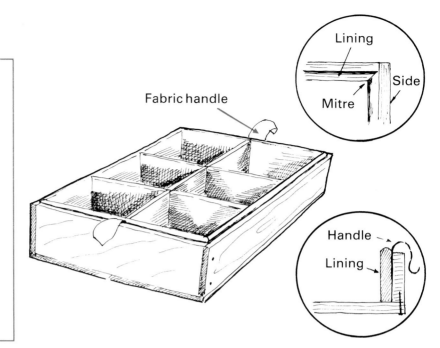

Fabric handle

Lining

Mitre

Side

Handle

Lining

Chisel cuts mitre

Fit the strips inside the tray. Fit them one at a time, each one fitting tightly into the corners. Then, remembering to handle the chisel carefully, chisel their ends so that the pieces meet at the corners at an angle. This is called mitring. Mitre each corner in the same way.

Divisions are fitted into shallow V-cuts marked with a knife and cut with a chisel in the edge linings. The end of each division is pointed and it slips into the groove. They are held in place with a spot of glue.

Chisel cuts 'V'

Knife cut

Lining

TAKE CARE!

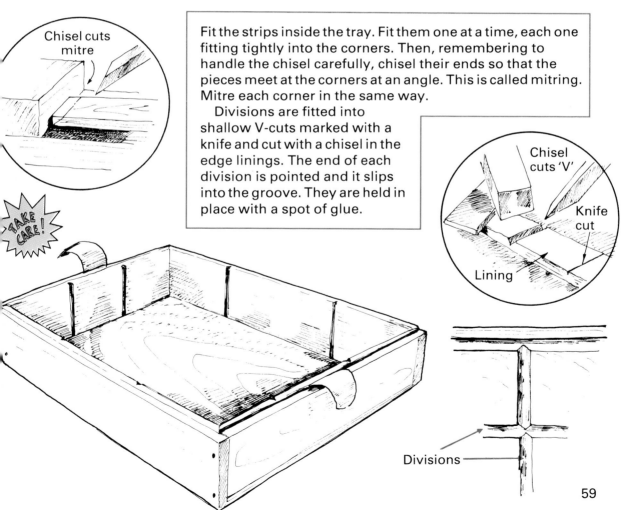

Divisions

A Work Box

Cut the wood roughly to size. Nail the front and back pair together with two veneer pins, and then trim them exactly to size with a tenon saw and shoulder plane. Repeat with the side pieces, checking they are square using a set square before drawing out the nails.

Mark off and saw off the drawer front from one end.

FRONT + BACK

SIDE

SIDE

DRAWER

Assembling

Assemble the box, using battens and string to hold it together while it is being drilled. Dismantle, and then glue and screw the box together, using countersunk brass screws. Position the screws to allow the top to be cut off. Check that the box is square, and correct it with battens if it has pulled together crookedly.

Fitting the top and bottom

Glue and screw the top. Space the screws evenly, and line up their slots. Glue the edges of the bottom plank, and hold it in place with panel pins.

Saw off the top, and plane around the edges.

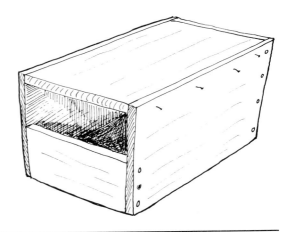

Saw off the top edges.

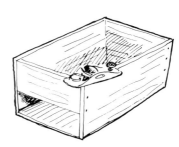

Fitting the inner floor

Take the untrimmed drawer sides, and prop them inside the box. Trim a floor plank, glue its edges, and lower it into position. Mark off, and then nail the floor with panel pins from the outside.

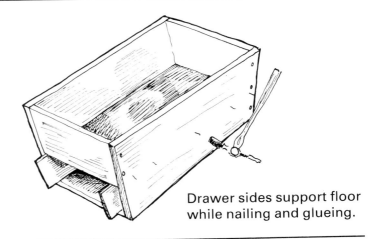

Drawer sides support floor while nailing and glueing.

Making the drawer

This is a long drawer. Trim the front to fit. Trim the sides, doubling piece, back and bottom, and check that they will fit inside the box. Assemble with glue and nails.

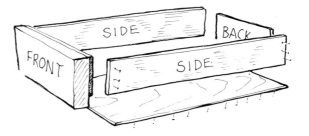

Fitting the trays

The trays rest on thin wooden strips, nailed and glued inside the drawer and inside the box. These strips allow the trays to slide, giving access underneath. Use a spacing block underneath the strip to keep the strips level when fastening them to the box.

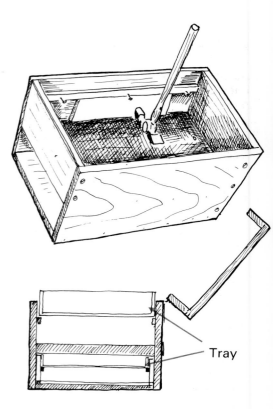

Trays

Make a tray for the drawer, and for the main box.

Tray

Hinges and hasps

'T' hinges would look nice. Screw them with roundhead screws to the back of the box. Then screw the hasp strap to the lid, and the staple plate to the box with countersunk screws. A dowel peg pressed through a hole in the floor of the box, at the back of the drawer, will prevent the drawer being pulled out until the padlock is unlocked, and the lid lifted.

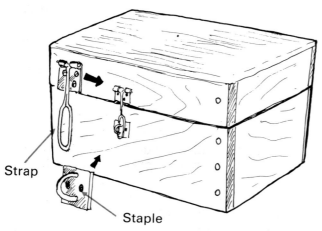

Strap

Staple

The box will look best if it is varnished. Sandpaper away all traces of the glue, and any roughness with 150 grit sandpaper, and stain the box with a rich brown stain wiped on with a cloth. When the stain is dry, put on a second coat avoiding the darker areas.

Leave the box to dry completely, before brushing on coloured varnish. Three coats should be enough to build up a bright shine. Finish by polishing the box with brown shoe polish.

Glossary

Across the grain At right angles to the lines of tree growth shown by the grain patterns on the plank.

Along the grain In the direction of the general grain pattern on a piece of wood.

Backing pad A block of stiff foam, cork, or wood used to support and hold flat a sheet of sandpaper.

Battens Narrow and straight strips of wood.

Bench Hook A wooden board which lodges against the edge of the bench, used to steady wood being sawn or chiselled.

Bevel A surface cut at a slant.

Blade The steel cutter of a plane, chisel, knife or saw.

Blade clamp Device for holding blade in a plane or saw.

Centreline A line drawn down the middle of a shape, from which measurements can be made, and against which templates can be positioned.

Chuck Cylindrical clamp which holds drill bit to the drill.

Chuck jaws Usually three steel fingers, mounted in the drill chuck, which close tightly around a drill bit.

Clamp Steel tool, with screw tightener, designed to squeeze pieces of wood together.

Countersink bit A wide pointed drill bit used for boring a conical recess in the wood for screw heads.

Countersink To sink a screw or a bolt head level with the wood surface.

Crank Handle with lever used for turning a drill.

Cross grain *See* across the grain.

Cutting board A board for cutting on to.

Cutting edge The sharpened edge of a chisel, plane or knife.

Diameter The width of a circle measured across its middle.

Doubling piece A decorative or reinforcing piece glued against a piece of wood.

Dowel A length of straight wood, cylindrical in shape. It can be bought in many diameters and lengths.

Drill bit A cutting tool for boring holes.

Emulsion paint Household interior wall paint with a matt finish. Not waterproof, but quick-drying on wood.

End grain The dull and rough wood exposed when a plank is cut across the grain.

File A steel blade with a roughened surface, used for shaping wood by abrasion.

Former A piece of wood which by its shape controls the shape of the finished woodwork built against it.

Framework A construction of parts which fit together.

Fretsaw 'V' A plank cut away to support work when fretsawing.

Gimp pins Short, flat headed nails.

Grain Marks and lines in the wood developed during tree growth. The grain patterns vary depending on the way the plank is cut, and the species of the tree.

Grit Abrasive particles glued to sandpaper.

Groove A channel carved in the wood.

Hand drill A small drill, powered by hand, which can drive a number of different sized drill bits.

Hollowing To scoop out with a gouge or chisel.

Mallet A wooden hammer for hitting the top of a gouge or chisel handle.

Marking out Accurate drawing on to the wood before cutting and drilling.

Mitring A joint between two pieces meeting usually at 90°. Each of the two pieces is cut to half the total angle.

Pad Scrap of wood used to protect work from the damaging pressure of the 'G' clamp.

Pilot hole A hole drilled into a piece of wood before screwing or nailing.

Pincers A gripping tool specially designed

for pulling out nails.

Pin hammer A light, long-handled hammer.

Pivot point The point around which a door or lid swings or hinges.

Plywood A board made from thin sheets of wood glued together.

Pre-drill To drill a piece of wood before screwing or nailing.

Punch To make a dent in the wood by tapping a nail into the surface. The dent makes an accurate point into which a drill can be pressed and started.

Right angle The angle formed between two flat surfaces meeting at 90° to each other.

Set The amount by which saw teeth are bent sideways to make room for the saw to glide through the wood.

Set square A marking tool giving an accurate right angle.

Shank The straight part of a nail or screw.

Shank hole A hole the diameter of the upper, unthreaded part of a screw shank, into which the screw will slip easily.

Shavings Thin ribbons of wood removed with a plane or chisel.

Shooting board A carefully constructed board which assists accurate edge and end planing.

Smoothing Removing roughness and levelling bumps.

Sole The flat underside of the plane through which the plane blade projects.

Splitting Forcibly tearing the wood apart along the grain.

Straight edge A long straight ruler or batten, used for marking straight lines.

Taper To become smaller towards the end, diminishing evenly.

Template A card or wooden shape used as a pattern for drawing around.

Veneer pins Very thin, small headed wire nails.

'V' groove A 'V' channel usually cut with a flat chisel, or a 'V' parting gouge.

Waste side The wood on the side of the marking line which is to be cut away, and goes to waste.

White spirit A clear liquid which dissolves, thins, and cleans off oil-based gloss paints. It is highly inflammable.

Wire nails Bought nails made from steel wire.